weight watchers®

.too~~l~~

for living companion

weight watchers®

for living tools companion

8 ways to get what you want

IDG Books Worldwide, Inc.
An International Data Group Company

Foster City, CA • Chicago, IL • Indianapolis, IN • New York, NY

IDG BOOKS WORLDWIDE, INC.
An International Data Group Company
919 E. Hillsdale Boulevard
Suite 400
Foster City, CA 94404

For general information on IDG Books Worldwide's books in the U.S., please call
our Consumer Customer Service department at 800-762-2974. For reseller information,
including discounts and premium sales, please call our Reseller Customer Service
department at 800-434-3422.

A Word about Weight Watchers

Since 1963, Weight Watchers has grown from a handful of people to millions of enrollees
annually. Today, Weight Watchers is recognized as the leading name in safe and sensible
weight control. Weight Watchers members form a diverse group, from youths to senior citi-
zens, attending meetings virtually around the globe.

Weight-loss and weight-management results vary by individual, but we recommend that
you attend Weight Watchers meetings, follow the Weight Watchers food plan, and partici-
pate in regular physical activity. For the Weight Watchers meeting nearest you, call
1-800-651-6000. Or visit us at our Web site at www.weightwatchers.com.

Weight Watchers Publishing Group
Editorial & Creative Director: Nancy Gagliardi
Senior Editor: Christine Senft, M.S.
Publishing Assistant: Jenny Laboy-Brace
Editorial Consultants: Palma Posillico, Jackie Raha
Text: Laurie Saloman
Illustrations: Rebecca Gibbon
ISBN: 0-7645-6132-4

BOOK DESIGN BY MICHELE LASEAU
LAYOUT CREATION BY HOLLY WITTENBERG

Manufactured in the United States of America

10 9 8 7 6 5 4 3

Table Of Contents

Introduction

8 Ways to Get What You Want

Congratulations! You've made a terrific decision—to join Weight Watchers to become a healthier, fitter person. Now that you've spent a bit of time learning about weight goals, the **POINTS**® Food System, and exercise, it's time to turn your attention to another valuable resource that will help you reach your goal and overcome any obstacles on the way—*the thinking and the feelings* behind your weight-loss efforts.

That's why we created the *Weight Watchers Tools for Living Companion*. They include:

Winning Outcomes: Know What You Want— To achieve your weight goals, you first need to know what they are. The Winning Outcomes Tool helps you identify exactly what you want to accomplish at Weight Watchers.

Empowering Beliefs: Believe It, Achieve It—Our beliefs strongly influence what we do. Learn how to believe in yourself and your ability to reach your goals.

Anchoring: Tap Your Inner Resources—Pick an anchor that will put you in touch with your inner resources any time you need them to keep moving toward your goal.

Storyboarding: Create a Path to Your Dream—A storyboard is a plan that shows the consecutive steps you need to take to achieve your goal. Just follow them and you'll be on your way to weight loss.

Mental Rehearsing: See It, Be It—Actors do it and you can, too. By practicing upcoming scenes in your imagination, you can achieve your desired weight-loss results.

Motivating Strategy: Feel Success *Now*—Focus on the wonderful feelings you'll have when you reach your weight goal, and get in touch with those feelings as you follow your eating and exercise plan.

Reframing: Change Your Mindset—Every behavior has a positive intention. The trick is to make your behaviors positive as well. Learn how to conquer bad habits and get the positive outcome you want.

Positive Self-Talking: Become Your #1 Fan—
Behind every winning team there's a motivating
coach. Learn how to be inspired by your own messages and you'll find yourself psyched to lose weight.

You may not even realize it, but you already have everything you need to make your dreams come true. The purpose of the Tools is to make you aware of all the resources at your disposal. There are reasons behind everything you do. You have choices, and you can learn from setbacks. Once you employ the psychology behind learning how to lose and keep off unwanted weight, you'll never feel in the dark again. You'll know how to anticipate situations, how to sail through difficult ones, and how to change gears if you feel you're getting off course. You are the master of your own destiny, and *Weight Watchers Tools For Living Companion* will show you how to make the most of yourself. Get set to open your toolbox!

1

Winning Outcomes:
Know What You Want

How many times a day are you called upon to decide what you want? Probably more than you think. Consider the choices that come with everyday living. Will you wear the blue dress to work? Will you go out for lunch? Then there are the weightier matters. What kind of car would you like to drive? Should you take a family trip to Disney World? If you're like most people, you spend a lot of time mulling over what you want. Think of how much time you spend each week flipping back and forth between television channels, unsure of what to watch. How long have you been weighing whether to stay in your job or look for a new one? It's as if you just don't know what you want!

We at Weight Watchers believe that knowledge is power—that is, knowing what you want gives you the power to get it. This is especially true when it comes to weight loss: If you want to achieve your health and fitness goals, you need to be clear about what they are. The Winning Outcomes Tool helps you determine what you really hope to accomplish, so you can make it happen! When you create a Winning Outcome, you set a goal for yourself that is:

- positive
- specific
- attainable on your own
- a good fit with your life

The Winning Outcomes Tool encompasses the who, what, where, when, and how of weight loss. A good example of a Winning Outcome might be this statement: I *(who)* want to shed pounds in a healthy way to keep up with my busy family. I'll join Weight Watchers *(what* and *where)* this week *(when)* and follow their weight-loss program *(how)*." This is an example of a long-term Winning Outcome—the desire to make a permanent lifestyle change in order to keep up with an active family. A short-term Winning Outcome might be: "I want to follow the Weight Watchers program so I can look good at my upcoming high-school reunion."

Make it a point to develop your Winning Outcome as soon as you can in your weight-loss journey. Then review it periodically to see if your goals have changed in any way. And don't forget to write down your Winning Outcome, because having it on paper will boost your chances of achieving it.

When Should You Create a Winning Outcome?

- When you need help identifying what you really want to achieve
- When your weight-loss results aren't matching your expectations
- When you need a push to get started on your weight-loss program

Winning Outcomes can help you...

...determine what you really want

It's been said that it's easier to move *toward* what you want than *away* from what you do not want. Of course, you know you don't want to be overweight. But try telling yourself that you're joining Weight Watchers because you want to be able to look in the mirror and smile at what you see. By spelling out a positive Winning Outcome, you will solidify what you want to achieve and arrive at your destination that much sooner.

...match your expectations to your dream

If you've been on the Weight Watchers program for several weeks and the scale has not shown the results you'd hoped for, you may be tempted to give up. *Please don't!* There are many more measures of success than just the numbers on the scale. By following the Weight Watchers program, you are making permanent, healthful changes to your eating habits; you are working toward feeling physically fitter and looking better; and you are learning to manage stress in your life without necessarily turning to food. Those are significant accomplishments! Remember, moving steadily toward your goal is more important than moving quickly. You may need to revise your Winning Outcome to include a more realistic time frame for your weight loss. This will help keep you on track and prevent you from getting discouraged.

...get started

For many people, the reason it's difficult to start a weight-loss program is because their goals are too vague. They know they want to slim down, but they haven't thought about why. Give your weight-loss wish some careful consideration. Do you want to drop pounds so that you can keep up more easily with your active, outdoorsy husband? Maybe you'd like to reduce your cholesterol. Or perhaps you want to shed post-baby pounds before you have another child. When you can pinpoint a reason for wanting to lose weight, you are much more likely to reach your goal. The key is to be specific about what you want.

HOW WINNING OUTCOMES CAN BE APPLIED IN YOUR LIFE

Now that you know what the Winning Outcomes Tool is all about, let's look at ways in which you can use it by showing how other members have applied it in their weight-loss quests. Here are the stories of Jim, Maris, and Mary Jo. Notice that although all are using Winning Outcomes with great success, they have applied the Tool in very different ways depending on their individual situations.

Achieving Success on His Own

Lisa usually prepares every meal for her husband, Jim, as she has since the day they were married. When Jim joined Weight

Watchers to lose 40 pounds, Lisa learned to count **POINTS** values to keep him within his range. But Lisa's job will take her out of town frequently for the next three months. Jim considers dropping out of Weight Watchers until she returns since he feels that he can't follow the program without her help. Jim's Leader reminds him that the Winning Outcomes Tool can help him keep his weight-loss outcome under his control. He revises his Winning Outcome so he can follow the plan without Lisa's help. He'll rely on frozen meals, and he'll eat out a few times a week with his Weight Watchers buddies.

Jim has transferred control of his success from Lisa to himself. This way he achieves success on his own and is able to keep going to meet his goal.

Setting a Positive, Specific Goal

Maris knew that she wanted to slim down, but she had neglected to set clear-cut goals for herself and, as a result, wasn't having much success. Once she joined Weight Watchers, Maris' Leader explained to her that if she set a specific goal she would be much more likely to achieve it. With her Leader's help, Maris crafted the following Winning Outcome: "1 will follow my Weight Watchers program this week and every week, including walking five days a week, so 1 can get down to 140 pounds, a healthy weight for me."

By nailing down the "who, what, when, where, and how," Maris has set—and is on her way to meeting—her desired weight goal.

Revising Her Goal to Fit Her Life

Mary Jo is fresh out of college and living in the city. She has a very active social life and a promising job in public relations, which means she attends a lot of catered parties and goes out to restaurants and clubs frequently. She joins Weight Watchers to lose 30 pounds, deciding that she's not going to eat out at all until she's proven herself by dropping the first 10 pounds. But since eating out is such a major part of her life, she finds she can't give it up for even a few weeks and is tempted to quit the program. She thinks about it again and decides that losing weight is too important for her health to put off on account of her job or her social life. Using the Winning Outcomes Tool, she adjusts her weight-loss goal so that it fits better with her life. She settles on a slower rate of weight loss than she originally had planned. Now she can eat out any time she likes.

Because Mary Jo has altered her weight-loss goal to better fit her on-the-go lifestyle, she is much more likely to achieve it.

A Member's Winning Outcome

When Ruth Greenwald received an invitation to join her daughter, son-in-law, and son-in-law's family on a Caribbean vacation this past winter, she knew right away that she would go. "I've always loved the sun, and I thought this would be a great way to spend time with my two-year-old granddaughter," says the schoolteacher and New York native. "The only problem was that I had gained a lot of weight over the years after I quit smoking, and was hesitant about putting on a bathing suit in front of my son-in-law's family."

When she mentioned her concerns to her hairdresser a few days later, he instantly knew what the solution was. "He said, 'Come to Weight Watchers with me tonight; the meeting is right near your house,'" Ruth recalls. "He had lost a lot of weight on the program and was very high on it. I figured I might as well give it a shot." Ruth went with her hairdresser that night, and when she got home she wrote out this Winning Outcome: "I will join Weight Watchers and follow their program so I can look and feel good for my Caribbean trip."

Soon Ruth was eating within her daily **POINT** range, exercising regularly, and watching the pounds melt off. "I had tried over the years to lose weight, but always halfheartedly," she admits. "Now that I knew I was going to be 'on display' at the beach, I was extremely motivated." By the time of the vacation three months later, Ruth had shed 26 pounds—and she's still losing. "I knew I could do it because I had spelled out my Winning Outcome. And a big bonus is that I had more energy than ever to keep up with my granddaughter!"

Chapter

2

Empowering Beliefs: Believe It, Achieve It

What are your strongest beliefs? They might be spiritual, emotional, medical, or philosophical. Do you believe in God, in love at first sight, in healing herbs, in ghosts? Whatever your personal beliefs, it's a good bet that your life is guided by them in many ways. That's because beliefs are ideas we think are true and that become a basis for our daily actions. Their power is such that we do things based upon what we do or do not believe.

Beliefs are so powerful because they live in our hearts as well as our heads. The Empowering Beliefs Tool can help give you the power to achieve your heart's desire. You're much more likely to succeed if you believe that:

- your weight goal is desirable and worth it
- you're capable of achieving your goal
- you deserve to reach your goal

As a member of Weight Watchers, your beliefs need to be in line with your Winning Outcome, and your Winning Outcome with your beliefs. Consider developing and strengthening your Empowering Beliefs about your weight goal as soon as you embark upon your weight-loss journey. They will help steer you toward your goal and keep you on track as you move toward it.

When Should You Use Empowering Beliefs?

- When you feel helpless
- When you feel hopeless about succeeding
- When you don't believe you deserve to reach your weight-loss goal

Empowering Beliefs can help you...

...determine how important your goal is to you

The only reason to work toward your weight goal is because it's important to *you*. It's wonderful to have a network of supportive family and friends, but you need to be doing this for yourself. You cannot work toward your goal solely to please someone else. Think about why losing weight is worth it to you. Perhaps when you achieve your goal you'll be a more patient person, able to perform better at your job and interact in a more satisfying way with your family. If your boss and family are happy that you lose the weight, that's great. But you can't succeed by doing it only for them—you need to do it for yourself, realizing it's important for *you* to feel healthier and more in control.

...realize that you are capable of achieving your goal

You undoubtedly have achieved far more in your life than you realize. You may have finished your degree, nurtured a loving

family, worked to buy your dream house, and landed that long-sought-after job. If you've managed to accomplish all that, certainly you will be able to lose the pounds you want to. Believe in your strengths. The same positive qualities that have helped you achieve what you wanted throughout your life will help you reach your weight goal now. If your goal seems too daunting, break it down into smaller goals. For instance, if you've got 50 pounds to lose, concentrate on losing 5 at a time. This way, your most immediate goal simply is to see the needle on the scale go down 5 pounds.

...realize that you deserve to achieve your goal

Make a list of everyone who appreciates you. This might include your spouse, your children, your friends, your boss— even your pet! Now think about why they appreciate you: your loving kindness, your friendliness, your dedication to a task all might be reasons. You've enriched their lives just by being you. Surely they would agree that you're deserving of the happiness you'll derive from reaching your weight goal. See yourself through their eyes as a deserving person. If you have trouble doing this, consider people you know whose lives will be enriched when they achieve their personal goals. Don't they deserve it? And if they do, why don't you deserve it, too?

HOW EMPOWERING BELIEFS CAN BE APPLIED IN YOUR LIFE

You now understand how the Empowering Beliefs Tool works, so let's talk about situations in which you could apply it to your own life. Following are the stories of Susan, Ed, and Maddie. Each of them used Empowering Beliefs to successfully work toward their personal Winning Outcomes.

Wanting It for Herself

Susan is 30 pounds overweight and unhappy about it. Her husband, Bill, would like to see her thinner as well and has been trying for months to convince her to join Weight Watchers. Susan decides to do it, but she doesn't lose any weight. She feels frustrated and helpless and quits the program. Finally she realizes that she joined Weight Watchers simply to please Bill because he wanted her to look better. After evaluating the reasons she herself wanted to lose weight—to have more stamina, to lower her cholesterol, and, yes, to look better—she rejoins Weight Watchers. This time Susan starts losing weight right away.

Susan has learned that the way to achieve weight-loss success is to want it for herself. Her Empowering Beliefs let her focus on why her weight-loss goal is desirable and worthy *to her*.

Being Capable of Achieving His Goal

Ed is working on losing 150 pounds. The task might seem overwhelming to someone else, but not to Ed. By using the

Empowering Beliefs Tool, he has learned to look at his other accomplishments in life for inspiration. He was a very successful student who now heads up his own high-tech computer company, and he has a wonderful wife and two fine sons. As a result, he tells himself, "If I can achieve all of that, I can lose the weight!" In the same way that he earned his graduate degree credit by credit and built his company product by product, he will focus on losing the weight pound by pound.

Ed has confidence in his ability to accomplish what he sets out to do. He knows goals sometimes must be achieved in stages, so he will take it step by step until he reaches his desired weight.

Believing That She Deserves to Be Thin

Maddie has been suffering from low self-esteem since her husband divorced her. She'd like to meet someone new, but her 20 extra pounds make her feel too self-conscious to express an interest in anybody—plus, somewhere inside she feels she doesn't deserve to look good. Maddie joins Weight Watchers and finds a sympathetic Leader who explains that she must regain enough self-esteem to feel she deserves to lose the weight. She goes home and makes a list of all the people who care about her and all the good things she's done for others lately. She gets together with friends who support her and want to see her happy. Once Maddie starts thinking about herself in a positive way and realizes that she deserves to do this for herself, she's able to start losing the weight.

Maddie's Empowering Belief that she deserves to shed the weight helps her see herself as a worthy person who has a right to look her best.

Chapter

3

Anchoring:
Tap Your Inner Resources

What happens when a ship drops anchor? The heavy anchor nestled into the ocean floor sends a signal to the ship to stop moving. Even a swift current is no match for the leaden weight that triggers the ship to a halt. Now imagine yourself as a buoyant vessel and the desire to overindulge in fatty foods as a current threatening to carry you away. Quick! You need to "drop anchor" to keep yourself steady. This is where the Anchoring Tool comes into play.

How does Anchoring work? Simply put, it lets you create personal cues and triggers that remind you of your Winning Outcome and put you in touch with the inner resources you need to achieve it. In the same way a lodged anchor sends a signal to a ship, your anchor will send you a signal that will help you move toward your goal. Your anchor can be an object, a word, a gesture, or a picture in your mind. When you need the strength to move against a current of temptation, you simply reach for your anchor to put yourself in a positive frame of mind.

Incidentally, there's nothing mysterious about Anchoring— it happens all the time without us even being aware of it. We automatically make associations between an experience and the things we see, hear, taste, smell, and touch while we're having that experience. As time distances us from the experience, something in our present environment can make us relive it.

The trigger might be a photo, a song, or a particular scent. The photo, song, and scent become "anchors" to the past because they bring us back to a certain state of mind.

When Should You Use Anchoring?

- When you don't think you have what it takes
- When you need to be reminded of your weight goal
- When you are overwhelmed by the challenge

Anchoring can help you...

...realize that you have the resources to meet your weight-loss challenge

When you feel that you don't have it in you to reach your goal, it's helpful to think back to a time when you achieved something you wanted. Perhaps you once served as mayor of your town. How did you go about winning the election? Were you determined? Committed? Driven? Think about how you felt when you reached this goal. Your next step is to choose an anchor and use it every time you want to remember how you felt while you were running for office. You might visualize your campaign poster to bring back that surge of positive energy so you can use it to achieve your weight-loss goal.

If you find it hard to stay on track toward your weight goal, you can use the Anchoring Tool to remind you of your priorities. For instance, if you consistently forget to record your **POINTS** during your busy workday, you might keep a small journal next to your telephone. This way, every time the phone rings or you start to make a call, you'll automatically be reminded to record your **POINTS** in the journal.

HOW ANCHORING CAN BE APPLIED IN YOUR LIFE

Now that you understand what Anchoring is and how to use it, you may be interested in learning how other Weight Watchers members have applied it with success. Here are Melanie's and Mary's stories.

Mustering Inner Resources to Achieve Success

Mary is a computer programmer with a high-stress job. Since she brings both breakfast and lunch to the office and is busy almost every minute of the day, she manages to stay within her planned **POINT** range. Every night on the way home from work, she plans dinner in her mind so she'll stick to her eating plan when she gets home. But once the dishes are done, she goes straight for the ice cream stashed in the back of her freezer as a way to unwind. Mary wants to change this behavior because it's wreaking havoc with her weight-loss efforts. She realizes that she needs a stronger commitment to her weight goal, and uses Anchoring to get in touch with this inner resource. Visualizing a time when her strong sense of commitment helped her complete her college degree at night, she decides to touch the ring on her finger to remind her of that achievement. Whenever she's tempted to go for the ice cream, she'll touch her ring.

Mary knows she's got it in her to achieve success. By using her ring as her anchor, she can reinforce her commitment to her goal whenever temptation hits.

A Clear Reminder Works Wonders

Melanie is overweight because she often digs into second portions out of habit. She decides to use Anchoring to change this behavior. She finds a picture of herself in a bathing suit when she was 40 pounds thinner and pastes it onto the table next to her dinner plate. She looks at it when she has finished one portion. Instead of reaching for a second portion, she leaves the table and puts her plate straight into the dishwasher.

Melanie relies on a visual image of herself at a desirable weight to remind herself to stop at one portion.

A Member's Anchor

When Debbie Sidway lost 66 pounds and reached her goal
weight last year, it was just the beginning of a new path to
self-discovery for the Connecticut native. Debbie had
always wanted to be a Weight Watchers Leader, and now it

looked like her dream might come true. But there was one problem: She was afraid to drive outside of her immediate neighborhood. "I was one of thirteen children, and the older kids were always taking the family cars," she remembers. "As a result, I never really got good at driving. When I became a stay-at-home mom, I drove to places like the library and grocery store—that was it." Debbie knew that to be a Weight Watchers Leader she would have to travel to multiple locations, some as far as 100 miles away. "I thought about not becoming a Leader simply because I was so afraid to drive," she recalls.

Debbie's revelation came the day she attended a tag sale and spotted a rhinoceros beanbag doll. "When I picked up that rhino, I suddenly had flashbacks of my childhood," Debbie says. "I remembered that my dad used to tell me rhinos had thick skin, were tough, and could do anything they put their mind to do. He would tell me I could be like a rhino and do anything I wanted to as well." Debbie bought the doll, named him Spike and decided he would be her anchor. "Whenever I looked at Spike, I remembered my dad's words and knew I could achieve my goal," she says. "So I decided to start driving all over. I put Spike on the dashboard and went. At first I didn't know which was north, south, east, or west. I was braking a lot and poor Spike was flying all around my car! I was so scared, but I had a dream of making a difference, and Spike gave me the power, strength, and thick skin I needed." Debbie has been a Leader for more than a year now, and she still keeps Spike in the car with her as her anchor.

4

Storyboarding:
Create a Path to Your Dream

Imagine you're a creative type in a high-powered ad agency. One of your assignments is to come up with a storyboard for a new toothpaste commercial. You put together a series of "panels" that depict the consecutive changes of scene in this commercial. Each action, such as a child uncapping the tube of toothpaste, brushing his teeth, then smiling at his mom, is featured on consecutive panels as a way to reach the goal—in this case, to convince an audience that the toothpaste is a winner and is worth buying.

At Weight Watchers, a storyboard is an action plan you create that outlines the consecutive steps you will take on the path to your weight goal. Each panel represents a specific step toward your goal. Each step is:

- stated in the positive
- within your control
- specific
- a good fit with your life

Let's say you want to get down to 140 pounds. Your storyboard might look something like this:

Step 1. Join Weight Watchers and become familiar with the program.

Step 2. Stock my kitchen with low-***POINT*** foods.

Step 3. Pay attention to my portion sizes.

Step 4. Walk 20 minutes a day at least four times a week.

Step 5. Write in my food journal every day.

Step 6. Attend my weekly meetings.

Step 7. Reach my goal weight of 140 pounds.

It might help you to actually make rough sketches of all the steps and tack them onto a piece of poster board. This can keep you on track toward your goal and help you see the process of losing weight as a series of manageable tasks. As with your Winning Outcome, it's a good idea to check your storyboard from time to time as you work toward your weight-loss goal to see if any changes need to be made. If so, you can add new steps to your storyboard or modify existing steps.

When Should You Use the Storyboarding Tool?

- When you don't know how to make your weight-loss dream come true

- If you usually lack follow-through when working toward your goals

- When your long-term weight goal seems too overwhelming

1. JOIN WEIGHT WATCHERS.

2. STOCK LOW POINT FOOD.

3. SMALLER PORTIONS

4. WALK 20 MINUTES 4 TIMES A WEEK.

5. WRITE IN JOURNAL EVERY DAY

6. ATTEND WEEKLY MEETINGS

7. REACH WEIGHT GOAL.

Storyboarding can help you...

...break down your long-term goal into smaller short-term goals

It's helpful to remember that there are two kinds of goals—long-term, which is your ultimate, final, or big-picture goal, and short-term, a smaller or interim goal. If the idea of losing 60 pounds (a long-term goal) seems overwhelming, concentrate on losing a smaller amount of weight, such as ten percent of your current body weight (a short-term goal). You can put together a storyboard that outlines the steps you'll take to get those first pounds off. When they come off, you're ready to take the next step.

...become more specific about how exactly to take the next step toward your dream

Now that you've joined Weight Watchers, you may be unsure of how to proceed. A storyboard can help you make the next move. For instance, you probably need to go to the supermarket and buy low-***POINT*** foods that will be the mainstay of your eating plan. Once you've done that, you might want to focus on your portion sizes. In this way, you will lead yourself through all the steps needed to reach your goal.

HOW STORYBOARDING CAN BE APPLIED IN YOUR LIFE

Here, two examples of how Weight Watchers members used Storyboarding to help them meet their weight-loss goals.

Mapping it Out

Karen is a young mother of three with 120 pounds to lose. She knows she is dangerously overweight and should slim down for her own sake and for the sake of her sons, but she feels completely overwhelmed by the task ahead of her. How will she do all the things she needs to do on top of caring for three very active children? Karen's Leader shows her how to put together a storyboard that outlines each specific step

Karen is to take to reach her goal. First, she will go to the supermarket one night by herself so she can focus on buying the most nutritious, low-*POINT* foods she can find. Then she will keep a journal within reach in the kitchen to track her *POINTS*. The next step is to trade baby-sitting favors with a neighbor so she can go out walking three times a week.

Since there are so many demands on her time, Karen needs to map out the specific actions she will take so she can stay on track toward her goal. With her storyboard in front of her, Karen finds it much easier to take the steps she needs to get there.

Breaking Down a Long-Term Goal

Ken often gets frustrated when he doesn't immediately achieve what he sets out to do. His goal is to lose 40 pounds, but after joining Weight Watchers his resolve starts to waffle. He has some low-*POINT* foods in the house that he eats for breakfast and lunch, but by dinnertime he starts thinking, "What's the use? Forty pounds sounds like a lot of work. I might as well just eat what I want." Ken decides to use Storyboarding to chunk down his 40-pound goal into smaller, 5-pound goals. He knows that with a little effort he can manage to lose 5 pounds, so he focuses on the steps he needs to take to achieve that goal. Once he has shed

5 pounds, his determination increases and he decides to go for the next 5 pounds. In this way, he reaches his goal.

Ken is using Storyboarding as a psychological tool to help himself deal with what he perceives as an overwhelming task. By breaking the task down into smaller chunks, he is able to tackle each one in succession.

Chapter

5

Mental Rehearsing:
See It, Be It

If you were called on to give a presentation at work, chances are you'd spend time rehearsing to prepare yourself for the event. You'd probably first practice delivering your presentation in front of a mirror, or perhaps before a small audience of trusted colleagues. You might not even recite any words at all but would instead run through the presentation in your mind as you went about your daily chores—in effect, you would *mentally* rehearse what you planned to say.

At Weight Watchers, we know that Mental Rehearsing can be an effective tool for weight loss. Since the mind and body work together, your mind can help prepare your body for a situation in which you want to behave or act in a way that will help you achieve your weight-loss goal. If you visualize the event—and how you will speak and act during it—you will be much more likely to meet your goal.

When Should You Use Mental Rehearsing?

- When you want to develop new, healthful behaviors
- When you need help dealing with an upcoming situation
- When you want to practice living like a thin person

Mental rehearsing can help you...

...make healthful behaviors part of your routine

The Mental Rehearsing Tool can help you make the right food choices on a regular basis. Think about your typical day and the situations that involve food. These would include mealtimes with your family but also could encompass coffee breaks at work or late-night TV viewing. Now run through your mind a picture of yourself going about your day. If you habitually reach for the box of donuts your teenage son insists on having at the breakfast table, instead imagine yourself entering the kitchen and going straight for the cereal shelf in the pantry. See yourself mixing a cup of high-fiber cereal with skim milk and some strawberries, then sitting down at the table to enjoy your meal with your family. If you normally opt for a high-fat mocha drink at the local coffee bar, instead visualize yourself ordering a regular coffee with skim milk, and then sipping it while you chat with colleagues. By preparing yourself mentally for potential minefields, you're much better able to sidestep any obstacles you encounter.

...prepare for an upcoming social event that's making you nervous

We all face difficult situations on the way to our weight goal. But since food and celebrating are such integral parts of our

culture, special events can be particularly challenging. If you're attending a wedding, holiday dinner, birthday party, or other event that features food, Mental Rehearsing can help you prepare yourself to stick to your eating plan. It also can help if you're worried that your efforts will be thwarted by others who urge you to indulge "since it's a special occasion." In preparation for an upcoming birthday party, for example, imagine yourself politely turning down the host's offer of cake and instead see yourself enjoying a tangy fruit salad and a cup of tea.

HOW MENTAL REHEARSING CAN BE APPLIED IN YOUR LIFE

Understanding how your mind can help you change your behavior is a key to weight loss. Let's take a look at how Amy uses Mental Rehearsing to stick to her eating plan when presented with her mother-in-law's mammoth meals.

Practice Makes Perfect

> It's Sunday afternoon, traditionally the time when Amy's family packs into the car and goes to Amy's mother-in-law's house for dinner. Her mother-in-law happens to be an outstanding cook who insists that her guests clean their plates and line up for seconds. Amy doesn't want to offend her mother-in-law, nor does she want to overindulge. Before arriving at the house, she imagines herself sitting down at the table. She takes small portions of several favorite foods.

Amy sees herself savoring the meal and engaging in happy conversation with her family. When she's finished and her mother-in-law starts to refill her plate, she imagines herself saying, "Oh, thanks, it was all so delicious but I couldn't possibly eat any more." To counteract any protests, Amy visualizes herself reaffirming her commitment to her eating plan and repeating, "I really can't manage any more, but it was wonderful."

Just as an actress needs to rehearse her lines before appearing in front of an audience, Amy realizes that she must rehearse her words and behaviors when faced with a well-meaning relative. Her mental practice sessions give her the resolve to act in a positive way week after week.

Chapter

8

Positive Self-Talking: Become Your #1 Fan

If you've ever watched a sporting event, you know that the coach plays a vital role in helping her team play effectively. As determined to win and as competent as the players may be, it's the coach who motivates them as she gathers them in a huddle, encouraging and cheering loudly. Her positive words spur the team to do the best job it can. In fact, a good coach can make all the difference between a winning team and a losing team.

Everyone needs encouragement to reach their goals, and Weight Watchers members are no exception. That's why we believe you must act as your *own* coach by using the Positive Self-Talking Tool. This becomes especially important if others are not supporting your efforts or, worse, are actively thwarting them. Since, like everyone else, you probably talk to yourself in some form or another, make an effort to choose positive, uplifting messages to send. Along with, "I've got to remember to buy milk," you can say, "I am working on becoming a healthier, happier person." See how easy it is? The words you speak to yourself help create your frame of mind, and if the words are positive and encouraging, you will be in a positive frame of mind to reach your weight goal.

When Should You Use Positive Self-Talking?

- If you constantly beat yourself up
- When friends and family put you down
- If low self-esteem leads you to eat
- If you've suffered a setback

Positive Self-Talking can help you...

...psyche yourself to lose weight

It can be discouraging to see your weight loss slow down, to hit a plateau, or even to gain back a few pounds. At times like this, you may feel frustrated and want to give up. Stop right there—you need a good dose of Positive Self-Talking to get yourself motivated again! Send yourself a message that will keep you going. By giving yourself the message that your goal is worth reaching and that you know you can do it, you put yourself into a state of mind that helps you achieve what you set out to do.

...defend against others who send you negative messages

As unfortunate as it is, sometimes people we care about don't support us in our weight-loss efforts. It can be especially hard to stick to an eating and exercise plan when people say things like, "I think you're thin enough already...want to have a piece of this cake?" or, "I don't know why you bother working out—it seems so pointless." At times like these, you have to muster your inner reserves of determination and send yourself some positive messages. Tell yourself, "If I stick to my eating and exercise plan, I'm one step closer to living the life I want for myself. It *is* worth it!" Even if you slip a little and have an extra helping of ice cream, you can remind yourself that you'll go back to your eating plan right away. Then do it! It also helps to make a list of all the successes you've achieved recently, even if they seem minor. This will keep you in an "achievement" frame of mind.

HOW POSITIVE SELF-TALKING CAN BE APPLIED IN YOUR LIFE

If it seems like Positive Self-Talking is somewhat like a pep rally, you're right! Take a look at how a couple of Weight Watchers members cheered themselves on to win the game of weight loss.

Coaching Herself to Win

Kathy is a Weight Watchers member who has 250 pounds to lose. She joined two months ago and so far has dropped 26 pounds. No one has noticed any change in her appearance. She's feeling frustrated by having to count **POINTS**, her weight loss is slowing down, and she realizes that at the rate she's going it could take three years to get to her weight

goal. But Kathy has discovered the power of Positive Self-Talking and isn't about to give up. She tells herself, "I need to do this to have the life I want, and I want to do it. It doesn't matter how long it takes. In three years I can be thin or still carry all this weight. Either way, three years will pass. Twenty-six pounds is a major step in the right direction. I'm doing all the right things. Soon enough, people will notice. And I already feel better."

Kathy has discovered the incredible power of cheering herself on. She knows that if she listens to herself, she will reach her goal. She has become her #1 fan.

Proving Herself Under Peer Pressure

Marie, a graduate student, has lost 20 pounds over the summer and needs to drop 20 more to reach her weight goal. When she goes back to school in September, all of her friends in the program tell her she looks great the way she is and not to lose any more weight. When the group goes out to lunch and Marie orders the lowest-*POINT* meals she can find, several of them make comments about "not enjoying herself anymore." When Marie invites her friends to spend two lunch hours a week going with her to the campus gym, she gets called an exercise fanatic. Although Marie is disappointed that her classmates aren't more supportive, she knows she's doing the right thing. She tells herself, "I can still be sociable and enjoy three meals a week with my friends as long as I stick to low-***POINT*** foods. It doesn't matter if they tease me for eating healthfully or for working out—I'm doing something great for myself and I know that in a few months I'll look and feel better than ever."

Peer pressure can be strong, which is why it's important to send yourself positive messages that support your own best interests. Although Marie is making an effort not to alienate her friends in her weight-loss efforts, she has put herself first because she values what losing weight will do for her.

When Jan Parcell's family heads for its favorite restaurant, the Geneva, the Illinois-based Leader practices what she calls her "virtual me" exercise. "My family always orders the chips and salsa appetizer," says Jan. "So before we get to the restaurant, I visualize myself staying away from the chips, drinking iced tea, enjoying the conversation, and relaxing. At the restaurant, I turn this visualization exercise into reality, and the chips are gone—finished off by everyone else—before I know it."

Jan got the opportunity recently to practice her Mental Rehearsing skills when a neighbor brought over a carrot cake as a thank-you gift. "I was *not* going to have that carrot cake," Jan remembers. "So I visualized myself ignoring the cake and instead eating a fat-free fudge bar. When I lived out this scene for real, I felt so great about myself. It was so empowering!"

As the mom of four young boys who like to snack, Jan faces temptation frequently—which is why she knows the importance of using the Mental Rehearsing Tool on a regular basis. "I could easily slip back into old behavior patterns," says Jan, who has maintained a 59-pound weight loss for more than a year. "I'm so glad I found something that keeps me on track."

6

Motivating Strategy:
Feel Success Now

Did you ever feel a surge of energy while considering something you wanted to do, a surge that made you just go for it? Perhaps you experienced this when you made the decision to join Weight Watchers—something from inside inspired you to take control of your weight. It could have been the certainty that you would feel more energetic after reaching your weight goal. It could have been a comment from an acquaintance that made you realize you'd let the extra pounds add up. Whatever it was, it motivated you to take the first step toward a fitter, healthier you.

When working toward your weight goal, it's important to experience in your imagination ahead of time all the good things that will be part of your life when you get there. This is the Motivating Strategy and it has the power to keep you going all the way to your goal. The key is to keep this experience of what is to come fresh in your mind whenever you feel your stamina flagging or your willpower wilting.

When Should You Use Your Motivating Strategy?

- If you've hit a plateau

- If you just want to give up

- When your goal seems too far away to be worth it

Your Motivating Strategy can help you...

...be reinspired by your reason for wanting to lose weight

When you first set your weight-loss goal, you had a motivation for doing so. Maybe you wanted to walk into an upcoming party wearing your best fitted black pantsuit, while all your friends told you how terrific you looked. To recharge your batteries, envision yourself at the party wearing the pantsuit. In this scene, not only are your friends showering you with compliments but even people you don't know are casting admiring glances your way. Let yourself experience the good feelings that come from having reached your Winning Outcome. Keep in touch with those good feelings as you count your *POINTS* and exercise regularly, and you will be reminded of why you're making the effort.

...break through a plateau in your weight loss

It can be hard to persevere in your weight-loss efforts when you don't feel you're achieving results. Using your Motivating Strategy during a plateau can make all the difference between breaking through it and giving up completely. First, congratulate yourself for having come as far as you have—whether you've lost 5 pounds or 50. Now focus on what you stand to gain by getting even closer to your weight goal. Picture it. Hear it. Feel it. Let yourself be energized by the thought of the

positive experiences to come once you've reached your goal. Focus on those feelings as you go about your day. Let them motivate you to continue with your weight-loss plan until you've pushed right past your plateau.

HOW THE MOTIVATING STRATEGY CAN BE APPLIED IN YOUR LIFE

Now that you have an idea how the Motivating Strategy works, learn how other Weight Watchers members have used the Tool to inspire themselves to take off the pounds.

Picturing the Good Life

High cholesterol and heart disease are a big part of Ellen's family history. Her doctor keeps telling her that regular exercise can help prevent these problems in Ellen's life. She knows that it would help her lose weight, too. But she doesn't seem to be able to motivate herself to get started, let alone maintain an exercise program. When Ellen's Leader talks about the Motivating Strategy during a meeting, Ellen realizes that this is what she needs. She imagines herself a year from now at her weight goal, full of energy because she's been exercising regularly. She thinks about all the things she's seeing, hearing, and doing at her weight goal that she wasn't able to do before embarking on her exercise program. She imagines what it feels like to be in such good shape.

Remembering these good feelings helps Ellen get started, and inspires her to stick to her exercise regimen.

Ellen has learned that experiencing how wonderful life can be when she's reached her goal is a powerful motivational tool.

Pushing Past a Plateau

Sophia knew her breaking point had come the day she put on her largest jeans and found that not only were they no longer baggy, they actually were too tight. She joined Weight Watchers, vowing to shed 35 pounds. About halfway to her goal, her weight loss started slowing down. Frustrated with the numbers on the scale, Sophia told herself it didn't matter since she had gotten halfway there and had already received compliments from people. She soon realized she was in danger of quitting the program. To motivate herself, Sophia pulled out her old jeans and put them on. They weren't tight anymore, but they were far from baggy. Sophia envisioned how good it would feel to slide on the loose jeans and pad around the house in them on rainy weekend afternoons. Thinking about that feeling gave her renewed energy to forge ahead toward her goal.

Sophia wisely employed the Motivating Strategy Tool to help her move past a weight-loss plateau. By reminding herself of why she wanted to get to her goal in the first place, she was able to find the energy to keep going.

Chapter

7

Reframing:
Change Your Mindset

Imagine you're shopping at a flea market and spot a landscape portrait that would be a perfect complement to your living room. You feel relaxed and serene just gazing at the mountain scene. The only problem is the frame—it's shoddy, cheap-looking, and the color is completely wrong. You decide to buy the painting anyway and reframe it in something that fits better with your decor.

As a Weight Watchers member, it's important to learn how to "reframe" a positive feeling with a positive behavior. If, for example, you overeat as a way to relieve stress and gain serenity, the Reframing Tool can teach you how to reach that positive feeling (serenity) by doing something better for yourself, such as walking, reading, or playing the piano. Your positive feeling is now "reframed" by a behavior that's good for you, much as the landscape portrait is reframed by something that fits well with the rest of the decor.

When Should You Use Reframing?

- When you want to shed an unwanted behavior

- If you eat when you are emotionally hungry

- If you are a stress eater

Reframing can help you...

...find a better way to get the positive feeling you want

Many experts in the field of psychology agree that there is a positive intention behind every behavior, even when the behavior itself is undesirable. This makes sense when you think about why you might be tempted to overeat. Maybe there is a lack of balance in your life. You work hard all day at the office, come home at night to cook for your family, and catch up with house chores after dinner. You never relax and pamper yourself—instead, you overeat. Wanting to destress certainly is a positive goal, but the behavior you've employed to reach it—overeating—is negative. The solution could be to "take five"—try sitting in a warm bath as you enjoy a delicious cup of herbal tea and your favorite book. This way, you get the positive outcome of relaxing without interfering with your weight goal.

...stop eating to fill an emotional void

Many people overeat because they feel lonely, tense, or depressed. The key is to identify what you get from overeating and find a new way to achieve that feeling. Instead of reaching for the potato chips when you feel depressed, think of other things you can do that will help lift your spirits. Have you ever been so involved in something that time just flew by?

Then that's the thing to focus on! If you loved working with watercolors as a student, go buy a set of watercolors, brushes, and an easel. Working on your art when you're feeling moody will elevate you to a whole new state of mind, keep you on your eating plan, and give you beautiful finished products to boot.

HOW REFRAMING CAN BE APPLIED IN YOUR LIFE

Need some real-life examples? Take a cue from Stu and Teresa, two Weight Watchers members who've put Reframing to use in solving their overeating dilemmas.

Relieving Boredom

Stu regularly sits down in front of the TV from 9:00 to 11:00 PM and completes a snacking marathon. He knows this isn't helping his weight-loss efforts, but he doesn't seem to be able to stop himself. With his Leader's help, Stu thinks about it and realizes that he has no other evening activities to keep him occupied—in effect, he is watching TV and eating as a way to relieve boredom. Stu makes a list of all the things in his life he has enjoyed, and discovers that there are several he can get involved in again. Since he dabbled in music at one time, he could enroll in a once-a-week music appreciation class after dinner. He also used to be a volleyball champ, so heading to the local Y for some informal night games is an

option. Whatever Stu decides to do, it should satisfy the positive intention—relieving boredom—that's behind his munching.

Stu has learned an effective way to replace an unwanted behavior with a positive one and still have the same outcome.

Finding New Ways to Be Sociable

Teresa, a young wife and mother, relishes her evenings with "the girls," her three best friends from high school. One of their favorite activities is spending evenings at each other's houses, watching videos and eating pepperoni pizzas. Teresa always organizes her daily *POINTS* so she can have two small slices of pizza at each of these gatherings. But when the pizzas arrive, she inevitably keeps munching right along with her girlfriends, often stopping only after three or even four slices. Teresa's Leader suggests that perhaps she is trying to avoid looking like a party pooper by overeating—after all, her friends don't stop at two slices. Teresa realizes she's right, and that this sociability is wreaking havoc with her eating plan. Teresa decides to stop at two slices. She'll keep the fun going by cracking jokes, giggling, and reminiscing with the group.

Once Teresa realized that the positive intention behind her pizza eating was to be sociable and not look like a stick in the mud, she figured out other ways to have a good time with her friends.

A Leader's Reframing Success

In this day and age, it's hard to escape stress. It lives—and thrives—at work and at home. For some people, stress is a small annoyance that rears its head every so often. For Penny Smith, a Leader from Spokane, Washington, it was much more of a problem. She was diagnosed with an anxiety disorder that can cause everyday situations and stresses to become overwhelming. Penny realized that when her worries became overwhelming, she often found herself in the kitchen. "I realized that I was eating as a way to 'shut off' my mind from my anxieties," she says. "If I was eating, I was thinking only about what to snack on next—not on the problem that had been bothering me before."

As a Leader, Penny knew about the Reframing Tool and thought it might be the key to keeping her eating and stress levels under control. A lifelong lover of crafts, she decided to set up several different workstations in her home that she could go to when her worries threatened to send her straight to the refrigerator. Now, if she needs to calm down, she picks a station and spends 20 to 30 minutes doing beading, stitchery, scrapbooking, or painting. "I get the mental recess I need, and my eating plan remains intact," she says. Best of all, the members in her group benefit from her artistic talents—Penny has created numerous gifts to reward them for their weight-loss successes!

Conclusion

Now that you're familiar with all of the Weight Watchers Tools for Living, it's time to put them to use! You may not need all of them, and you'll probably use different Tools at different times in your weight-loss journey. The important thing is that you've gained an understanding of the "why" and "how" behind losing weight. Knowing yourself and how you think *can* and *will* make all the difference in your weight-loss efforts.

We hope you've enjoyed learning about the Tools, and we wish you success in reaching your goals. We're always here for you at Weight Watchers!

Notes

Notes

Notes

Notes